RAINBOWS BOOK OF PROMPTS

LILY LAWSON

THE
WRIGHT HOUSE

Published by
The Wright House.

CONTENTS

The document or notebook is open. A fresh blank page awaits your brilliance. And … nothing. The time you have found in your hectic schedule to write is being frittered away by staring at the screen or notebook or off into the distance. Your imagination is not coming up with the goods. What to do?

Abandon the attempt and occupy yourself with one of the thousands of things on your to-do list? Or find a way to fire your imagination so this time can be spent as you intended? Tempting as it is to walk away, and you may indeed choose that path, you have to ask yourself if that will fulfil you as a writer, because being a writer means putting words on a page.

Whether you write every day or whenever you can squeeze it in, the important thing is to write in the time you have given yourself, whether you feel inspired or not. It doesn't matter if the set up isn't perfect. You need to focus on what's important and that's getting words on the page.

This book is designed to help you do that. In these pages you will find a range of prompts (starting points) to get you thinking and other helpful suggestions.

When deciding what to include, I attempted, as much as possible, to use words or phrases that had more than one interpretation. If you write them on a piece of paper, or in a new document and brain dump whatever connections you can make, you might find there's more than one direction to go. Combining random ones can lead to some unexpected places.

You might start at the beginning and work your way through, or open at random whenever the need arises. It may be that you favour a particular type of prompt or mix two or more together.

There is no right or wrong way to use this book. It's completely up to you.

Believe in yourself. You can do this.

NOTES

TOOLS

I thought it might be helpful to give you some tools to use with these prompts. These are just suggestions. You may enjoy them as exercises, adapt them to better meet your needs or ignore them all together.

These can be used independently or together.

Freewriting

The idea is you write whatever immediately comes to mind when you consider the prompt word or words. Do not stop or self-edit – just keep writing until you run out of ideas. It doesn't have to make sense or be in sentences or have punctuation. It's just a way of brainstorming to see where it leads to.

Lists/Bullet Points

Another technique is to write the prompt at the top of the page and make a list or a set of bullet points that you associate with it.

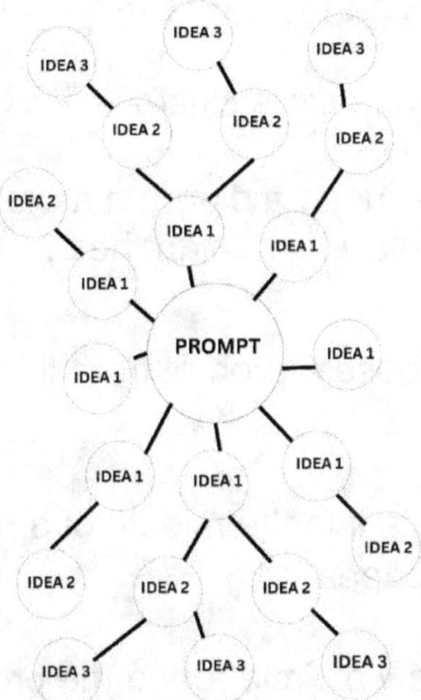

Key –

Idea 1 is the idea you get from the prompt

Idea 2 is the idea from the prompt plus idea 1

Idea 3 is the idea 1 plus idea 2

Clustering

How to make a cluster –

I've included a diagram as an example which might help.

a. Choose a prompt from this book.

b. Write it in the middle of a piece of paper.

c. Draw a circle round the prompt.

d. Write in the space around the circle anything the prompt word makes you think of.

e. Draw a circle around each idea separately.

f. Connect the new circles to the original circle with a line or arrow.

g. Write in the space outside of the new circles anything those ideas make you think of.

h. Draw circles round anything that doesn't have a circle round it.

i. Draw lines or arrows to link the new circles to any other circles which contain the same or similar ideas.

j. Repeat steps g to i until you run out of time, paper or ideas.

There are no limits to how many branches you can make or directions you can take. Branches can be as long or as short as they need to be. The diagram is a starting point. Yours will look different.

The exercise is to spark ideas which may lead to poetry, fiction or non-fiction or some other creation or can be used as a warm-up exercise before you write something else.

You can also use this method if you get stuck by placing the problem in the centre circle and thinking of all the possible options of where the story could go.

SECTION ONE

NOTES

ONE WORD AT A TIME

PART ONE

- Access
- Face
- Selcouth
- Outrage
- Kismet
- Chopsticks
- Treason
- Nebulous
- Ascertain
- Curtail
- Mine
- Surface
- Groove
- Fragment
- Speck
- Yield
- Hurdle
- Galvanise
- Quiver
- Relay

- Charge
- Imitate
- Concur
- Solemn
- Proscribe
- Tempt
- Vacuum
- Grandiose
- Quake
- Infiltrate
- Abject
- Juxtapose
- Beset
- Righteous
- Trust
- Evaluate
- Season
- Nexus
- Diminish
- Overt
- Contact
- Hide
- Divert
- Pendulum
- Attention
- Gallery

THREE LITTLE WORDS
PART ONE

- Fridge, fur, frank
- Karate, kitten, kiwi.
- Hit, hire, hill.
- Move, munch, marble.
- Balloon, basket, baseball.
- Alligator, ashes, aubergine.
- Miss, kiss, bliss.
- Cheer, beer, deer.
- Jump, jelly, jinx.
- Those, nose, dose.

- Robust, routine, run.
- Swing, bring, ring.
- Quick, quaint, quack.
- Flash, cash, mash.
- Visit, victory, value.

SOMETHING DIFFERENT
PART ONE

What happened in this photo?

What's the story here?

Photo Credits J.C. Paulson

I'LL THROW YOU A LINE
PART ONE

- They woke up on a bench.
- At the top of the hill.
- He opened the bag.
- The door was ajar.
- In the middle of the road.
- There was no card.
- A bag of sweets.
- The door was locked.
- She wrote her name.
- The smell was overpowering.

- He played the violin.
- There was a party.
- A marble rolled across the floor.
- Smoke filled the room.
- He lit a fire.

PLACE, CHARACTER, THING.

PART ONE

- Moon, snowman, tulips.
- Park, architect, chocolate.
- Garden, hairdresser, watch.
- Swimming pool, panda, shovel.
- Golf course, zookeeper, book.
- Racetrack, florist, fork.
- Theatre, footballer, plate.
- Cinema, gymnast, spoon.

- Pet shop, driving instructor, popcorn.
- Motorway, giraffe, cup.
- Bookshop, clown, crisps.
- Casino, nurse, ketchup.
- Office, weightlifter, bowl.
- Marina, lighting technician, laminator.
- Squash court, delivery driver, curtain pole.
- Water slide, fire fighter, trolley.

THAT'S MY LINE
PART ONE

Excerpts from **SANDCASTLES,**
a short story collection,
by Lily Lawson.

A glove-wearing human.

She is falling
and I can't stop her.

Love's got nothing to do with it.

A vaguely familiar hand.

Zero response.

Sodden missiles of rubbish.

I am with you always.

Hunger filled his body.

This is another kind of war.

I open my mouth to shout.

She wasn't going anywhere.

Retrieve the contents.

FISTFUL OF RANDOMNESS
PART ONE

- Carrot, random, steel, token, weave.
- Apple, strange, carriage, use, deter.
- Sauce, varied, silence, match, pinch.
- Dates, wide, pour, meek, need.
- Turnip, fantastic, detest, busy, lick.
- Mustard, bare, text, coach, lie.
- Pear, fun, tonne, coin, stun.
- Cucumber, similar, create, aria, punch.

- Figs, high, defy, jolly, want.
- Melon, familiar, craft, post, rash.
- Parsnip, wander, enjoy, tire, strip.
- Jam, swerve, cut, past, mould.
- Turmeric, demonstrate, store, throw, banal.
- Asparagus, filtration, gem, dual, investigate.
- Basil, hydration, reserve, mirage, endeavour.
- Chive, enrage, diplomacy, attract.

MUSICAL INTERLUDE
PART ONE

- If Paradise Is Half As Nice – Amen Corner.
- Walking On Broken Glass – Annie Lennox.
- Too Late For Goodbyes – Julian Lennon.
- Good Vibrations – The Beach Boys.
- Wouldn't It Be Good? – Nik Kershaw.
- That Don't Impress Me Much – Shania Twain.
- They Can't Take That Away From Me – Frank Sinatra.

- Shake It Off – Taylor Swift.
- The Land Of Make Believe – Bucks Fizz.
- Summertime Blues – Eddie Cochran.
- Come As You Are – Nirvana.
- Purple Rain – Prince.
- For What It's Worth – Buffalo Springfield.
- Who Wants To Live Forever? – Queen.
- Won't Go Home Without You – Maroon 5.
- You Give Love A Bad Name – Bon Jovi.

COMMONLY CONFUSED WORDS
PART ONE

Write something for each set of words using them all correctly.

There, their, and they're

Their means something or someone belonging to a person or persons.

There is a place where something is located.

They're is a contraction of they are.

Write, rite and right

Write is to form words on a surface.

Rite is a prescribed form or manner governing words or actions for a ceremony.

Right is conforming to facts or truth.

Quiet and quite

Quiet means little or no noise.

Quite can mean very, completely or entirely.

Formally and formerly

Formally describes things done in an official way.

Formerly means prior to this time.

NOTES

STRENGTHEN YOUR WORDS
PART ONE

Write something using the first word, then replace that word with the second one.

INSTEAD OF	TRY
Large	Vast
Small	Minute
Book	Reserve
Doorway	Entrance
Ordinary	Mundane
Remember	Recall
Last	Final
Ate	Consumed

Chance	Opportunity
Tell	Divulge
Stop	Prevent

THIS MIGHT HELP
PART ONE

- Write about your procrastination, how it makes you feel, and what you are worried about.
- Write a list of rhyming words.
- Try writing in a new location.
- Pick a machine and think about how you would manage to complete its functions without using it.
- Read a magazine, newspaper, or blog.
- Talk to someone.
- Write a plan to teach someone something you know how to do

well as if they have never heard of it before.

- Set a timer for five minutes and write a hundred random words.

- Do a quiz online or from a book, watch a quiz show or attend a quiz night.

- Choose something you know nothing about. Set a timer and see what you can find out.

- Read a poem.

- Imagine you had no internet connection. How would that change your day/week/month/year?

FRIENDS' PROMPTS
PART ONE

"Success and jealousy. Reputation and obscurity.
Love and hate.
Fury."

Adam's Witness – J. C. Paulson

"Frogs and alarm clocks."

Frogs and Alarm Clocks – Ken Paulson

"The silver South Seas pearl necklace on the marble bathroom countertop guaranteed Megan success. It's always worked in the past."

Letters from Shadow Oaks — K. L. Small

"She glanced back at the note. Why was this happening? Anne

read the message, “Remember who you are.”

Nadira’s Storykeeper – Tanya Packer

“The lights flickered and a loud thundering roar exploded like a bomb. “

Nadira’s Storykeeper – Tanya Packer

“The students all stepped back. Their eyes darted around, searching to find the one playing the trick.”

Nadira’s Storykeeper – Tanya Packer

SECTION TWO

NOTES

ONE WORD AT A TIME
PART TWO

- Stake
- Pander
- Junction
- Varsity
- Aisle
- Vent
- Eliminate
- Fortitude
- Stretch
- Tender
- Hack
- Outlying
- Stupefy
- Peregrinate
- Accrue
- Continuous
- Lament
- Vine
- Flourish
- Bequeath

- Simpatico
- Yeoman
- Vein
- Ignite
- Temerity
- Byzantinize
- Nascent
- Abandon
- Hubris
- Vicissitude
- Boojum
- Ward
- Nemesis
- Result
- Egregious
- Lubricate
- Devalue
- Trickle
- Ferry
- Converse
- Spoke
- Peer
- Land
- Complex
- Upturn
- Level

THREE LITTLE WORDS
PART TWO

- Deed, need, feed.
- Grate, fate, late.
- Book, look, nook.
- Ought, organ, outdoor.
- Stand, star, sink.
- Dwindle, swindle, kindle.
- School, fool, cool.
- Mug, tug, hug.
- Zip, zoom, zigzag.
- Hung, rung, sung.

- Mark, lark, spark.
- Young, yellow, yield.
- Spun, fun, bun.
- Penny, pretty, panic.

SOMETHING DIFFERENT
PART TWO

Show Don't Tell:

If I write 'leaves skittered along the pavement' you can work out that it's windy, even though I didn't say so.

Write two or three sentences that convey a thunderstorm is happening, WITHOUT using the words: thunder, lightning, storm.

P. S. C. Willis

'"A weaver. A long tale affixed in thread, a banner of human life," the Auctioneer said. "She will sew a wondrous story for her owner, or they may cut her life like the finest of threads and enjoy a brief respite from the weariness of history."'

From the POV of your character, what story does the weaver pick out?

The Hiding – Alethea Lyons

"She stared into the depths [of the crystal ball], unblinking, willing something, anything, to happen."

What would your character see in a crystal ball?

The Hiding – Alethea Lyons

I'LL THROW YOU A LINE
PART TWO

- The blanket caught fire.
- The handle came off.
- There was a note.
- She blocked his way.
- They lost an oar.
- An elephant was in the hotel.
- The platform was full.
- He held his breath.
- They walked towards her.
- At the bottom of the lake.

- The sun obscured her vision.
- It was made of chocolate.
- He knocked at the door.
- She drank it all.
- They started to play.
- The picture fell off the wall.

PLACE, CHARACTER, THING.

PART TWO

- Hospital, dog, omelette.
- Dentist, van driver, sausages.
- Church, mailperson, torch.
- Vets, singer, chips.
- Library, tightrope walker, chandelier.
- DIY store, figure skater, lightbulb.
- Trapeze, otter, traffic cone.
- Café, refuse collector, bookends.

- Graveyard, DJ, pen.
- Roof, dancer, paper.
- Garage, vet, paperclip.
- Community centre, mechanic, jug.
- Ice rink, steeplejack, thermometer.
- Jetty, chimney sweep, wok.

THAT'S MY LINE
PART TWO

Excerpts from
MY FATHER'S DAUGHTER,
a poetry collection,
by Lily Lawson.

If time allows.

To give rise to old thought.

I tried on identities.

You give me hope.

I know you'll never leave.

Standing like a barrier between us.

In its all-encompassing arms.

The sunlight through the windows.

Happily sharing the limelight.

My companion on my travels.

The reminder of the day.

What we found on holiday.

FISTFUL OF RANDOMNESS
PART TWO

- Syrup, walk, envy, twist, skill.
- Lemon, cold, write, battle, instil.
- Peppers, sing, avoid, royal, step.
- Spices, leave, dictate, smile, tenet.
- Berries, dance, evade, legal, ape.
- Vinegar, linger, change, frown, event.
- Radish, evolve, cover, heat, ski.

- Annise, free, lank, soar, begin.
- Cabbage, rotate, speak, rip, foam.
- Lemongrass, roll, dry, glue, form.
- Honey, jump, dye, paste, stripe.
- Walnuts, rigid, dictate, spend, travel.
- Celeriac, fright, romance, slit, web.
- Fennel, glimmer, physics, kneed, splinter.
- Bratwurst, horizon, reference, majesty, knell.

- Gateau, heist, chemistry, revere, ounce.

NOTES

MUSICAL INTERLUDE
PART TWO

- The Tide Is High – Blondie.
- Murder On The Dancefloor – Sophie Ellis Bextor.
- I Heard It Through The Grapevine – Marvin Gaye.
- All Day And All Of The Night – The Kinks.
- Forever In Blue Jeans – Neil Diamond.
- Hooked On A Feeling – Vonda Shepard.
- Stairway Of Love – Marty Robins.

- Great Balls Of Fire – Jerry Lee Lewis.
- Chocolate Girl – Deacon Blue.
- The Sun Always Shines On T.V. – A-ha.
- Paper Heart – Lucy May.
- Truly Madly Deeply – Savage Garden.
- The Sound Of Silence – Simon And Garfunkel.
- Emotional Fire – Cher.
- Just Around The Hill – Sash!
- Will You Still Love Me Tomorrow? – The Shirelles.
- I'll Be Around – The Spinners.

- Wind Of Change – Scorpions.
- Under The Boardwalk – The Drifters.
- Should I Stay Or Should I Go – The Clash.
- Bitter Sweet Symphony – The Verve.
- Yellow Submarine – The Beatles.
- My Ever Changing Moods – The Style Council.
- Why Does It Always Rain On Me? – Travis.
- Tell Laura I Love Her – Richie Valens.
- Life In One Day – Howard Jones.

- Shape Of You – Ed Sheeran.
- Look For The Good – Jason Mraz.
- Dancing On The Ceiling – Lionel Ritchie.
- Once Upon A Time In The West – Ennio Morricone.
- Everybody Wants To Rule The World – Tears For Fears.
- On Days Like These – Matt Monro.
- How Long Will I Love You? – Ellie Goulding.

COMMONLY CONFUSED WORDS
PART TWO

Write something for each set of words using them all correctly.

Poll and pole

A pole is a long straight thing often made of metal which can be placed in the ground to hold something up.

A poll is where a number of people are asked a question or questions to get their collective views on a subject.

Dessert and desert

Dessert is something sweet you eat at the end of a meal.

Desert is a very hot dry area of land usually covered with sand or to leave a place.

Lose and loose

Loose refers to something that is not securely attached.

Lose means not being able to find something or someone.

STRENGTHEN YOUR WORDS
PART TWO

Write a sentence using the first word, then replace that word with the second one.

INSTEAD OF	TRY
Told	Informed
Regular	Consistent
Dry	Arid
Wild	Uninhabited
Hide	Conceal
Good	Beneficial
Bad	Wicked
First	Primary

Smell	Aroma
Leave	Depart
Came	Approached

THIS MIGHT HELP
PART TWO

- Write someone else's to-do list –

  a pirate, a neighbour, shop assistant, delivery driver, a superhero, a dog, a cartoon character.

- If a friend was stuck, what advice would you give?

- Try writing in offline/online/on your phone whatever is different for you.

- Write a letter to someone.

- If you were in charge of the world, what changes would you make? List them.

- Write a list of movies you want to see and say why.

- Write as if it's one hundred years in the future.

- Write about an experience you had as if it happened to someone else.

- Write with someone else.

- Pick an object and list as many uses as you can for it.

- Choose theme songs for your friends/family/colleagues/neigh bours.

- Watch TV/a movie.

- Read a book.

FRIENDS' PROMPTS
PART TWO

"Then they heard someone yell "wait!" followed by the sound of a gunshot."

The Traveler on the Train – K. T. McGivens

"Her body flowed like hot butter as she walked, stopping both men and women in their tracks."

The Passing of Preston Peabody – K. T. McGivens

"These days it's hard to know your friends from your enemies."

The Secret at Sunset Hill – K. T. McGivens

"But, somewhere deep in the recesses of his soul, he knew that he was glad that she was still single."

The Secret at Sunset Hill – K. T. McGivens

"On impact, his hand shifted slightly, giving her the chance to bite down hard on his index finger."

The Incident on Ivory Island – K. T. McGivens

"Don't let anything bad ever happen to you," she whispered. "I won't be able to bear it."

The Ransom for Ruth Reed – K. T. McGivens

"He sat up suddenly. Tightly swathed in bedsheets and sweat."

Haft – Alexandra Peel

“There is usually no evidence to either prove or disprove these theories,” she said.”

Haft – Alexandra Peel

““I’m a rabbit!” Anne declared.”

The Floating Church – Alexandra Peel

“…people who travel around pick up peculiar habits.”

The Floating Church – Alexandra Peel

“There was a familiar scratching outside the window.”

A Boxful of ‘Christmas’ Shorts – Alexandra Peel

“Just before the match went out, I saw him smirking with amusement, or pleasure.”

The Life and Crimes of Lockhart and Doppler – Alexandra Peel

““Gosh, you are big.” I remarked.”

The Life and Crimes of Lockhart & Doppler – Alexandra Peel

SECTION THREE

NOTES

ONE WORD AT A TIME
PART THREE

- Core
- Liquify
- Phlizz
- Harangue
- Sporadic
- Patch
- Align
- Sui generis
- Insurrect
- Tangent
- Faith
- Brouhaha
- Mentor
- Atone
- Convert
- Glass
- Benefit
- Spacearium
- Pitch
- Introduction

- Sharp
- Complete
- Hesitate
- Tenebrous
- Asportation
- Fiddle
- Enemy
- Prize
- Canard
- Trenchant
- Switch
- Information
- Alarm
- Shock
- Rizz
- Arboricide
- Squash
- Vociferous
- Ectopia
- Scunner
- Beneficence
- Diglot
- Lugubrious
- Proof
- Fuse
- Church

THREE LITTLE WORDS
PART THREE

- Unite, untie, uniform.
- Ice, ink, incredible.
- Detect, blaze, jaded.
- Edge, egg, escalate.
- November, nut, nimble.
- Lift, love, live.
- Salmon, keyboard, marsh.
- Curtain, blab, quick.
- Devolve, trace, hoop.
- Fragment, circle, enslave.

- Judge, dank, coast.
- Nectar, grieve, pitch.
- Announce, dangle, thunder.
- Quest, badger, sling.
- Welcome, jiggle, nape.
- Detract, elect, bedeck.

SOMETHING DIFFERENT
PART THREE

Where is this?

What's happening?

Who lives here?

What's their story?

Photo credits Alethea Lyons

I'LL THROW YOU A LINE
PART THREE

- She slid down the hill.
- The road was icy.
- Fog filled the town.
- There were no books.
- He was on the roof.
- The bridge was out.
- At the bottom of
  the swimming pool.
- They tried to stop the bus.
- A sheep was in the bedroom.
- The roads were jammed.

- The playground was closed.
- He couldn't stop laughing.
- She climbed the hill.
- They hailed a cab.
- It had rained for days.
- They bought ice cream.

PLACE, CHARACTER, THING.

PART THREE

- Locker room, lizard, double bass.
- Furniture store, gardener, compass.
- Lighthouse, librarian, tape measure.
- Cake shop, curtain fitter, chalk.
- School, electrician, dustbin/trash can.
- Post office, poet, jellybeans.
- Train, penguin, lollipop.
- Van, politician, chair.

- Bed, snake, radiator.
- Car park, crocodile, spanner.
- Restaurant, scientist, violin.
- Coach station, journalist, drums.
- Fishmongers, manicurist, Allen key.
- Roundabout, potter, crayons.
- Hard Shoulder, owl, timer.
- Pier, childminder, golf ball.

THAT'S MY LINE
PART THREE

Excerpts from
***A TASTE OF WHAT'S
TO COME*** a poetry collection,
by Lily Lawson.

The vivid colours of my life.

Beyond the pages of a book.

You hide your magic.

Deprived of human touch.

Why can't people get it?

I am not sure that I love you.

It is your truth
so you must tell it.

Give me a world.

I'm thinking it might be
where I belong.

Cloud your vision.

Taking a somewhat
broader view.

FISTFUL OF RANDOMNESS
PART THREE

- Banana, wonderful, teach, libel, maroon.
- Cardamon, astonish, wet, staple, risk.
- Squash, hop, range, total, pump.
- Peach, amazing, tutor, donate, even.
- Butter, believe, mutter, petty, lift.
- Tomatoes, skip, alter, tempt, press.
- Salt, visit, crest, freeze, atone.
- Rhubarb, stay, code, chill, wild.

- Nutmeg, banish, spear, incite, relay.
- Cauliflower, run, splash, tear, loan.
- Pineapple, vamp, pause, confuse, tilt.
- Jelly, grill, tell, liaison, minor.
- Potatoes, narrow, call, hatch, sway.
- Strawberry, sour, wither, pass, value.
- Cheese, doubt, manage, pretty, labour.

MUSICAL INTERLUDE
PART THREE

- Puppet On A String – Sandie Shaw.
- You Spin Me Round (Like A Record) – Dead Or Alive.
- The River Of Dreams – Billy Joel.
- Swinging On A Star – Bing Crosby.
- Bad Connection – Yazoo.
- It Wasn't Me – Shaggy.
- Blueberry Hill – Fats Domino.
- Do You Really Want To Hurt Me? – Culture Club.

- Justified And Ancient –
  The KLF.

- Walking Back To Happiness –
  Helen Shapiro.

- She's Electric – Oasis.

- Slipping Through My Fingers –
  Abba.

- Stranger On The Shore –
  Acker Bilk.

- All Of Me – John Legend.

- Till The Rivers All Run Dry –
  Don Williams.

- Come On Eileen –
  Dexys Midnight Runners.

- Heaven Is A Halfpipe – OPM.

- Love Lies Lost – Helen Terry.

- Rock Around The Clock – Bill Hailey And His Comets.
- When You're Looking Like That – Westlife.
- Singin' In The Rain –- Gene Kelly.
- Wind Beneath My Wings – Bette Midler.
- Hasn't Hit Me Yet – Blue Rodeo.
- Skyline Pigeon – Elton John.
- Under The Moon Of Love – Showaddywaddy.
- Town Called Malice – The Jam.
- Losing My Religion – R. E. M.
- What Is Love? – Haddaway.

- All Of You – Silk Stockings.
- Spirit, Body And Soul – The Nolans.
- The Boy Does Nothing – Alesha Dixon.
- Bed Of Roses – Bon Jovi.
- Love Is All Around – The Troggs.

COMMONLY CONFUSED WORDS
PART THREE

Write something for each set of words using them all correctly

Pore and pour (verb form)

Pore means to read or study something very carefully.

Pour means to transfer something often liquid from or into a container.

Horde and hoard

Hoard refers to a hidden amount of something valuable.

Horde refers to a large group of people.

Stationery and stationary

Stationary means not moving or changing.

Stationery refers to materials used for writing, typing or similar.

STRENGTHEN YOUR WORDS
PART THREE

Write a sentence using the first word, then replace that word with the second one.

INSTEAD OF	TRY
Dug	Excavated
Bite	Nibble
Show	Demonstrate
Fetch	Retrieve
Try	Attempt
Mix	Combine
Varied	Eclectic

Cut	Slice
Keep	Retain
Join	Connect

THIS MIGHT HELP
PART THREE

- Write a stream of consciousness about your day – What happened? How do you feel? What are your thoughts?

- Try writing at a different time of day.

- Write a list of books you want to read and why.

- Pick a building and list as many uses as you can for it.

- Go for a walk.

- Listen to the radio.

- Learn something new.

- Look at homes for sale online imagine living in them.
- Write about today as if it was one hundred years ago.
- Do something you've been putting off.
- Imagine you are lying on the ground and can't get up what happened? What difficulties do you face? What can you do? What can you see? How does it feel?
- Join the library/download a library app.
- Pick an animal and write from their point of view.

FRIENDS PROMPTS
PART THREE

"The chill she carries from the river settles deep into her soul."

River Witch – Cheryl Burman

"Her dreams are of fire and water."

River Witch – Cheryl Burman

"A soft white light glowed through her fingers like an old-fashioned glowstone."

Winter of the White Horde – Cheryl Burman

"She waved the rod and vanished in a smoky black cloud."

Winter of the White Horde – Cheryl Burman

"Two days from the castle, she had spent the first night in a barn, no sign of the farmer, his family or livestock."

Winter of the White Horde – Cheryl Burman

"I'm not sure if I can come back from this, the ultimate betrayal. I have always felt ambivalent towards the woman who gave birth to me but was incapable of raising me. I honestly don't think I can continue being a part of our bogus relationship."

Just Say It – Tessa Barrie

"But none of that really matters, Lucy. Material things in life just don't matter. It is the people who are important. Always remember that."

The Secret Lives of the Doyenne of Didsbrook – Tessa Barrie

"Kaz curls around me. There are advantages to being a short person in a tall person's world."

About Charlie – J.M. Langan

"Am I just a girl in a painting, is the girl in the painting even real?"

About Charlie – J. M. Langan

"The city hasn't come to life yet. The odd car passes her, she ignores it."

Puca –The Solstice Baby – J. M. Langan

"I'll always remember the first day I saw her; the woman who made me, at least temporarily, forget that I had been married to the woman I loved for ten wonderful years. She was reading a book, and I think that's what caught my attention to be honest."

Unforgettable – R. E. Loten

"Across the aisle, a little way down the carriage, a man sat silently observing them."

The Reign Of The Winter King – Henrietta Edwards

SECTION FOUR

NOTES

ONE WORD AT A TIME
PART FOUR

- Swell
- Authority
- Conceit
- Harridan
- Boundary
- Askance
- Mint
- Palooka
- Keel
- Hitch
- Stun
- Drift
- Divulge
- Pierce
- Lavish
- Rock
- Pontoon
- Grizzle
- Varlet
- Fizzle

- Gleed
- Bilge
- Handle
- Fret
- Alert
- Bemuse
- Truckle
- Compete
- Minutes
- Accelerate
- Emit
- Fillet
- Philofelist
- Epitome
- Recede
- Flinch
- Omit
- Crack
- Abide
- Market
- Penalty
- Sack
- Jamboree
- Disquiet
- Ablute
- Aptitude

THREE LITTLE WORDS
PART FOUR

- Dive, linger, intake.
- Evolve, squall, throw.
- Manure, glory, sharpen.
- Hesitate, destroy, kerfuffle.
- Include, hassle, bellow.
- Obviate, shore, curfew.
- Protrude, nudge, wallow.
- Govern, jazz, hollow.
- Blast, accuse, motor.
- Shot, neaten, breach.

- Bloom, jagged, fallow.
- Loom, skip, roar.
- Bleak, wrangle, swallow.
- Reduce, march, sown.
- Deter, abbreviate, intrude.

SOMETHING DIFFERENT
PART FOUR

Sensory detail:

Use the room you are in, or a preferred story setting and brainstorm as many sensory details as you can. For example what can you

SEE?
SMELL?
TOUCH?
FEEL?
TASTE?

Spend five minutes writing as many examples for each as you can.

Now, spend ten minutes writing a scene where you draw on these sensory details, trying to include at least one of each.

P. S. C. Willis

“There was nothing special about it being the autumnal equinox. She wouldn’t meet anything supernatural in the Shambles.' Write a scene of a time and/or place where it feels like something magical is about to happen.

The Hiding – Alethea Lyons

I'LL THROW YOU A LINE
PART FOUR

- There were thousands of pens.
- Wind whipped the trees.
- A kite lay on the ground.
- They were stuck.
- He had no appointment.
- The cupboard was empty.
- She wasn't invited.
- The suitcase was empty.
- She opened the parcel.
- They lay on the beach.

- He walked in the parking lot.
- The lights went out.
- He made the presentation.
- They were locked in.
- The temperature dropped.

PLACE, CHARACTER, THING
PART FOUR

- Train platform, drummer, rubber bands.
- Hotel, tortoise, hammer.
- Car, engineer, chopsticks.
- Lake, police officer, table.
- Bowling alley, frog, milkshake.
- Call centre, lifeguard, chair.
- Bank, chef, diamond.
- Cabin, doctor, sword.
- Sea, cat, trumpet.

- Riverbank, photographer, set of weights.
- Cave, sailor, saxophone.
- Duck pond, software developer, socket set.
- Backstage, ecologist, shoelaces.
- Allotment, quarterback, needle.
- Shoe shop, baseball player, emerald.
- Yacht, juggler, ice cream

THAT'S MY LINE
PICTURE BOOKS

Excerpts from ***IF I WERE INVISIBLE …*** a picture book by Lily Lawson.

If I were invisible …

I'd have more time to play.

Dance in the rain.

Look at the stars.

Excerpts from
THE PALM TREE SWINGERS ISLAND BAND,
a picture book,
by Lily Lawson.

This was no time for the glums.

Took the roof right of the place.

You didn't have to be there.

They really were quite famous.

FISTFUL OF RANDOMNESS
PART FOUR

- Sesame, revolve, tactic, impasse, sweat.
- Cream, remove, notch, strong, graze.
- Yam, kneel, pint, entry, star.
- Fries, evolve, tight, forgive, quiver.
- Sprouts, beautiful, smash, innocent, joust.
- Orange, weird, iron, purloin, tower.
- Hamburger, revere, forget, quack, bow.

- Cucumber, cuddle, cotton, cute, cite.
- Ketchup, reverse, regret, quake, endow.
- Maple, address, wail, tumble, entrust.
- Gorge, grant, gather, granola, gravitate.
- Yeast, regulate, appal, rumba, twirl.
- Fennel, admire, aria, waltz, scrunch.
- Lime, hot, writhe, goal, pluck.
- Noodles, lucid, rotation, navigate, string.

MUSICAL INTERLUDE
PART FOUR

- The Way You Look Tonight – Tony Bennett.
- Looking For Linda – Hue And Cry.
- Better Together – Jack Johnson.
- You'll Never Walk Alone – Gerry And The Pacemakers.
- Pipes Of Peace – Paul McCartney.
- The Man Who Sold The World – David Bowie.
- A Teenager In Love – Dion And The Belmonts.

- Invisible Touch – Genesis.
- It's Five O'Clock Somewhere – Alan Jackson.
- 24 Hours From Tulsa – Gene Pitney.
- Wish You Were Here – Pink Floyd.
- Sit Down, You're Rocking The Boat – Guys and Dolls.
- Just The Way You Are – Billy Joel.
- Fall Into Me – Forest Blakk.
- Stand By Me – Ben E King.
- Eyes Without A Face – Billy Idol.
- Uptown Funk – Mark Ronson.

- Who Slapped John? – Gene Vincent.
- Who Knew? – Pink.
- A Kiss To Build A Dream On – Louis Armstrong.
- Together Forever – Rick Astley.
- Rockin' All Over The World – Status Quo.
- How Do I Say Goodbye? – Dean Lewis.
- The Boy Is Mine – Brandy And Monica.
- Alive And Kicking – Simple Minds.
- Fade Into You – Mazzy Star.

- In The Air Tonight – Phil Collins.
- Feeling Good – Nina Simone.
- Raindrops Keep Falling On My Head – B. J. Thomas.
- I Don't Want To Miss A Thing – Aerosmith.
- Sealed With A Kiss – Bryan Hyland.
- Cupid – Sam Cooke.
- Somewhere Only We Know – Keane.

COMMONLY CONFUSED WORDS
PART FOUR

Write something for each set of words using them all correctly

Plain and plane

Plain means lacking decoration or pattern or a flat piece of land with no trees.

A plane is an airplane/aeroplane or a tool or the use of same in carpentry.

Flout and Flaunt

Flout means to openly disregard, such as a law or convention.

Flaunt is to display something in order to attract attention.

Access and excess (noun)

Access means a place of entry.

Excess is an amount more than necessary or desirable.

Peace and piece

Peace means the end of war or a state of calm.

Piece means a part, amount or type of something.

STRENGTHEN YOUR WORDS
PART FOUR

Write a sentence using the first word, then replace that word with the second one.

INSTEAD OF	TRY
Find	Locate
Turn	Rotate
Draw	Sketch
Change	Alter
Swap	Replace
Leave	Depart
End	Abolish
Good	Beneficial

Kind Benevolent

THIS MIGHT HELP
PART FOUR

- Become the character of a writer just for the day. Imagine 'the writer' is writing the story. 'The writer' could be a famous writer, a writer you know or an identity you create.

  This doesn't mean changing your author name. It's up to you whether or not you tell anyone. It's sometimes easier when you feel imposter syndrome coming on to distance yourself from the story and treat the writer part of you as separate from the rest of you. Giving that part a name can make it feel like a role you can pick up and put down as necessary.

- Imagine you are being interviewed what questions

would you like to be asked and how would you answer them?

- List what you would take if you were going on a writer's retreat. Describe what happens when you're there.

- Write a list of people you want to meet and why.

- Write a list of places you want to go and why.

- Copy someone else's writing routine.

- Imagine you are building a city. What would you include?

- Take part in a writing challenge/class/competition

- Join a writing group.

FRIENDS’ PROMPTS
PART FOUR

“I have never liked hats and to tell you the truth, they don't like me.”

Sky Watcher: A Shadow in Time – Heather Lynn

“I heard her suck in her breath; her eyes were wide. “Like magic?””

Sky Watcher: A Shadow in Time – Heather Lynn

I stood on his feet, glad that I’d worn my soft little shoes.

Sky Watcher: A Shadow in Time – Heather Lynn

“The only conclusions I could come up with were that perhaps in a given situation, there is only one choice to be made; or, events that are not within our control will happen, events that none of our decisions would or could have changed."

Sky Watcher: A Shadow in Time – Heather Lynn

Then I heard a door open, and by the squeak that it made, I knew it was the door to my room. What on Earth are they doing in my room?

Sky Watcher: A Shadow in Time – Heather Lynn

"What we do here ain't always pretty, but it's necessary." Hammer talked while Jeff continued to gaze out the window. "I understand being an idealist. I do. Believe it or not, I used to be one myself. The world isn't black and white, though. If you're going to hang with us, you gotta ask yourself at the end of the day, 'Did I do more good than bad today?' If that answer is yes, then that's all you need. If it's not, then maybe

Jen was wrong about ya, and you find yourself another gig."

Z.E.R.O. – Jessica Ungeheuer

"We don't need tragedy to make us feel alive. We need happiness. We need peace. In our minds, as well."

Tangle of Choices – Eve Koguce

"Look about you, take courage, they are nearer than you think..."

Joseph's Coat –
Vastine Bondurant

"All roads out of hell lead home."

Joseph's Coat –
Vastine Bondurant

NOTES

SECTION FIVE

NOTES

ONE WORD AT A TIME
PART FIVE

- Avuncular
- Spine
- Current
- Jack
- Investiture
- Tease
- Menace
- Event
- Dispatch
- Assert
- Ludicrous
- Curious
- Sting
- Nocturnal
- Attach
- Taint
- Pinion
- Dragoon
- Jaunty
- Qualm

- Lodge
- Fence
- Target
- Scrunch
- Construe
- Panache
- Mollify
- Hunch
- Belie
- Abet
- Hackle
- Pinnacle
- Crew
- Shackle
- Organ
- Shiver
- Belittle
- Natant
- Chutzpah
- Austerity
- Thrill
- Velocity
- Tawdry
- Myology
- Banal
- Decree

THREE LITTLE WORDS
PART FIVE

- Revamp, alfresco, symphony.
- Tune, valid, wither.
- Rash, myth, diplomat.
- Click, option, attend.
- Morsel, bedraggled, decant.
- Dignity, plethora, loaf.
- Jollification, morale, decadent.
- Hobnob, infiltrate, slide.
- Astound, quiver, insurgent.
- Vandal, languish, convene.

- Future, shift, machine.
- Hook, theatre, abound.
- Piece, letter, field.
- Concave, insolent, emergence.
- Askance, board, sage.

SOMETHING DIFFERENT
PART FIVE

What's the story?

Why is someone here?

Photo credits Alethea Lyons

I'LL THROW YOU A LINE
PART FIVE

- Ask the question.
- It's a snake.
- Tie it tight.
- It's a mystery.
- It kept spinning.
- On the roof.
- She arrived breathless.
- The doorbell rang.
- There's no obligation.
- When summer ends.

- They knocked it down.
- The ladder fell.
- He looked sad.
- She was happy.
- Up a tree.
- Under the bed.

PLACE, CHARACTER, THING
PART FIVE

- Fairground, IT consultant, billiard balls.
- Seaside, elephant, marshmallows.
- Forest, fire eater, apple.
- Motorbike, acrobat, cricket bat.
- Zoo, referee, football.
- Ferry, teacher, snooker cue.
- Gym, dinosaur, blueberries.
- Museum, pilot, kiwi fruit.
- Art gallery, zookeeper, shelf.

- Cable car, unicorn, harp.
- Library, lighthouse keeper, stopwatch.
- Pavillion, swimmer, coffee.
- Harbour, paediatrician, ruby.
- Yard, optometrist, sapphire.
- Antique shop, hockey player, coving.

THAT'S MY LINE
THE RAINBOW SERIES

Excerpts from
RAINBOW'S RED
BOOK OF POETRY,
a poetry collection,
by Lily Lawson.

I weave through hate and love.

We paint from the palette of life.

Every nuance of your being.

The richness of this existence.

When the first sign
of light breaking.

My spirit responds.

Fate's dice roll separates
life and death.

Help is on its way they say.

Tattered ends of
unfinished tasks.

You sense every weakness.

The temporary pause
before reality.

Tomorrow waits
in a different land.

Excerpts from ***RAINBOW'S ORANGE BOOK OF POETRY***
a poetry collection,
by Lily Lawson.

I am humbled by your mastery.

Destroyed, evolved,
or laid to waste.

Gratitude seeps from
my every pore.

When human consolation
turns its back.

Its aroma stretches
beyond its presence.

Punctuate my silence.

The language of the long dead.

In secret code.

Waiting for me up ahead.

To not use it is a crime.

Sprinkle them with magic.

Beyond the point of gratitude.

Excerpts from ***RAINBOW'S YELLOW BOOK OF POETRY***
a poetry collection,
by Lily Lawson.

Demands we must address.

It took an unexpected shape.

Days of unmovable existence.

A moment that might alter fate.

The spell has not worn off.

Bring forth change.

Warriors of space and time.

Always free to all.

Constant reinvention.

It fits quite well.

There are no easy answers.

Out here in the wild.

FISTFUL OF RANDOMNESS
PART FIVE

- Cinnamon, grab, honest, stall, tumble.
- Dip, drive, deliver, drop, divulge.
- Tofu, grid, bag, exit, forget.
- Saffron, spurn, acacia, salsa, thatch.
- Chestnut, regurgitate, prefund, curtsey, straw.
- Scone, churn, dismiss, unearth, sofa.
- Grapes, full, learn, mull, cherish.

- Broccoli, low, wail, guilt, stash.
- Custard, elope, discover, mist, stove.
- Biscuit, dismay, uncover, fathom, wood.
- Grapefruit, disquiet, salve, latch, plug.
- Cake, abscond, hatch, sole, base.
- Pasta, clean, reprimand, hover, kindling.
- Lolly, divert, match, hark, length, cloud.
- Meringue, concoct, lament, entrap, sky.

MUSICAL INTERLUDE
PART FIVE

- Mack The Knife – Bobby Darin.
- If I Was - Midge Ure.
- Goodnight Girl – Wet Wet Wet.
- I Walk The Line – Johnny Cash.
- The Love Shack – The B-52's.
- That's Not My Name – The Ting Tings.
- Chantilly Lace – Big Bopper.
- Starmaker – Kids From Fame.

- Accidentally In Love – Counting Crows.

- Blue Suede Shoes – Elvis Presley.

- Love Resurrection – Alison Moyet.

- Dancing In The Moonlight – Toploader.

- Party Up The World – D:Ream.

- All Around The World – Lisa Stansfield.

- Hit The Road, Jack – Ray Charles.

- Be My Downfall – Del Amitri.

- I Still Haven't Found What I'm Looking For – U2.

- Born To Be Wild – Steppenwolf.
- One Call Away – Charlie Puth.
- Tracks Of My Tears – Smokey Robinson & The Miracles.
- China In Your Hand – T'Pau.
- You Can't Hurry Love – Diana Ross And The Supremes.
- Talking To The Moon – Bruno Mars.
- Save Your Kisses For Me – Brotherhood Of Man.
- Four Letter Word – Kim Wilde.

- What Took You So Long? – Emma Bunton.
- Tonight Is Forever – Pet Shop Boys.
- Born Too late – The Poni Tales.
- Thunderstruck – AC/DC.
- Love Is Strange – Mickey and Slyvia.
- The Final Countdown – Europe.
- In The Still Of The Night – Fred Paris and The Satins.
- How Deep Is Your Love – The Bee Gees.
- White Flag – Dido.

COMMONLY CONFUSED WORDS PART FIVE

Write something for each set of words using them all correctly

Statue, stature and statute

A statue is a figure often a person or animal made of stone, metal or similar.

Stature can be about a person's height or a level of respect for a person.

Statute refers to a written rule or law.

Preposition and proposition

A preposition is used with a noun, pronoun or noun phrase to show location, direction or time or to introduce an object.

A proposition is a plan or offer that is presented to a person or group to consider.

STRENGTHEN YOUR WORDS
PART FIVE

Write a sentence using the first word, then replace that word with the second one.

INSTEAD OF	TRY
Wide	Extensive
Funny	Amusing
Stay	Remain
Mix	Combine
Dear	Expensive
Like	Resembling
Close	Adjacent
Roomy	Spacious

Words	Vocabulary
Moved	Relocated
Grumpy	Irritable

THIS MIGHT HELP
PART FIVE

- Write a list of people and what you value about them.
- Imagine you are starting a company what would it be? Who would you recruit? Why?
- Join a book club.
- Take a character and write their background.
- Use any book title in this book as a prompt.
- Make some food differently even if it's just a sandwich.

- Think of as many things as possible beginning with a letter of your choice.

- If you could be part of a story which story, who would you be and what would you do?

- Rewrite any extract from this book in your own words.

- Ask the same question to a number of different people and note the answers.

- Draw something

- Write about your day as if you lived in a different location.

FRIENDS' PROMPTS
PART FIVE

Stories are like time travel.

Time Traveling for Dummies – Rue Sparks

We've all felt what it's like to be immortal, if only for a moment.

The first seconds after we lose someone whose heart we grew roots together with. The feeling of those hands and roots grasping our own torn away, leaving only thin strands that decay with time.

That is immortality.

The empty and cold space their absence leaves. Knowing that hole may be refilled, yet nothing will ever again fit together with us in the same way.

In that moment we taste immortality. The knowledge that they are gone…and we are not.

"Our lives are not one moment of shattering, and remaking. The breaking never ends so long as we breathe. Life is decay and slow or sudden motion."

Hubris – Rue Sparks

"I knew my role in this story before I had the language for it. Who knows what history will call you and I, who will be labeled the hero or villain in their collective memory. All I can do is what I believe is right."

“Consider that your penicillin is my arsenic, and that our bodies can sometimes metabolize the poison or neutralize the cure.

“What a curse it is, to be the villain or hero in turns.

A contradicting narrative. A Venn diagram without intersection. Either end of the metronome's swing, in time with the beat of the universe.

Perhaps death is forgiveness, then. That we don't live to see the breadth of the ripples of our actions.

But not for you. The only solace that awaits you is the slow heat death of the universe by inches.

Perhaps nothing was meant to be immortal. Even the fabric of existence wears thin with time. As do you."

Love Story of a Hero and Villain – Rue Sparks

NOTES

SECTION SIX

NOTES

ONE WORD AT A TIME
PART SIX

- Decry
- Aisle
- Create
- Swell
- Prompt
- Switch
- Inept
- Fecund
- Baste
- Vacuum
- Season
- Powder
- Vine
- Retinue
- Tongue
- Quantum
- Twist
- Expiate
- Ward
- Gadfly

- Trust
- Ridge
- Charge
- Festoon
- Love
- Brevity
- Incubate
- Sliver
- Adept
- Tangent
- Patch
- Stun
- Crew
- Emblazon
- Prolong
- Virtue
- Longevity
- Reck
- Defraud
- Hyaline
- Wound
- Jurisprudence
- Endeavour
- Fumble
- Sporadic
- Endear

THREE LITTLE WORDS
PART SIX

- Fete, hue, grapple.
- Obliterate, lure, jazz.
- Abandon, bejewel, grave.
- Mere, lease, turret.
- Dunk, armour, easel.
- Import, cuff, dilute.
- Pitcher, amore, truant.
- Articulate, bevel, staunch.
- Funk, ramshackle, grace.
- Lore, delicate, ease.

- Myth, justice, gravel.
- Imprison, nuance, turquoise.
- Gunk, shackle, eager.
- Exhort, parole, rotund.
- Felony, swing, hitch.

SOMETHING DIFFERENT
PART SIX

A writer's toolbox contains description, dialogue, action, and introspection.

For example, when applying these to coffee, we get:

Description: Beads of condensation slid down the bevelled sides of the tumbler as the iced coffee sat on the table.

Dialogue: “Can I have some sugar for this?” she asked the waiter, gesturing to her iced coffee.

Action: She took a sip of the iced coffee, wincing at the bitter taste.
Introspection: Coffee was bad for her. Sugar was bad for her. But nothing else could cut through the

muggy July day and the poor sleep of the previous night the same way.

Choose an item, action or person.

You can use coffee or one of your own choosing.

Write one sentence each for…
Description:
Dialogue:
Action:
Introspection (thoughts and feelings):

These don't initially need to flow logically one after the other, though they should all be about the same thing.

Rearrange and add to them as needed to make them flow smoothly.

P. S. C. Willis

"The shabby little room is sparsely furnished. In one corner, there's a wooden chair and two small tables just large enough to provide a resting place for the smoking oil lamps that light the room, and on the wall hangs a hideous still life depicting a vase of waxy flowers with a dead pheasant lying next to it. None of this really registers. All I see is the bed."

Describe a room or location in detail, then pick something in it for your character to focus on and explain why.

Journeys: The Archers of Saint Sebastian – Jeanne Roland

“In the centre of the library, a horse chestnut tree rose to the domed glass ceiling. Its roots slithered across the floor and its trunk rose from the stacks, through the central librarians’ desk in the main reading room. Its canopy spread under the myriad colours of the stained-glass roof.” Imagine a place you go to frequently and place it in another world e.g. past, future, alien, magical.

The Hiding – Alethea Lyons

"The moon hovered behind naked silhouettes of trees and stars twinkled through their branches like an adornment of fairy lights. Frolicking stars, fallen from the sky, flickered around the trunk of an old oak, illuminating a skirt of long grasses. Then the tree was gone, consumed by the unending darkness." Describe a scene your

character sees from a car window?
Write a flash story about magic and nature.

The Hiding – Alethea Lyons

NOTES

I'LL THROW YOU A LINE
PART SIX

- Write it down.
- And then what?
- It ends here.
- They ate it.
- I'm not surprised.
- Hold me back.
- The phone rang.
- Under the stars.
- A hole appeared.
- A free pass.
- I can't stop.

- The card read.
- It starts today.
- It ends tomorrow.
- There’s little time.

PLACE, CHARACTER, THING
PART SIX

- Rodeo, typist, brick.
- Office, sailor, water pistol.
- Football ground, tailor, thesaurus.
- Cricket ground, airman, dictionary.
- Furniture shop, spy, parachute.
- Boatyard, opera singer, rice.
- Dressmakers, vicar, triangle.
- Bridal shop, mascot, handbells.

- Fast food restaurant, captain, flute.
- Market, astronaut, cello.
- Aquarium, fashion designer, trombone.
- Bingo hall, conductor, pasta.
- Stadium, bingo caller, glockenspiel.
- Helicopter pad, archer, ice pick.
- Runway, concierge, table runner.
- Court room, linguist, placemat.

THAT'S MY LINE
SANTA BOOKS

Excerpts from
SANTA'S EARLY CHRISTMAS,
a picture book,
by Lily Lawson.

Well, he had a good excuse.

They went down a treat.

He seemed to be quite dizzy.

He couldn't stay awake.

Excerpts from
SANTA'S HUNGRY CHRISTMAS,
a picture book,
by Lily Lawson.

He'd be late for his first stop.

There was too much work.

Eager to get away.

It was time for some fun.

FISTFUL OF RANDOMNESS
PART SIX

- Revolve, incite, pour, dictate, abdicate.

- Stir, contribute, quantify, dart, pyramid.

- Commune, diameter, wicked, myriad, nuclear.

- Empathy, legislate, position, deconstruction, frost.

- Obedience, postpone, swallow, demystify, turbulence.

- Magnificent, transport, vexed, hollow, devalue.

- Ritual, propose, shallow, dedicate, morose.

- Solidify, dishevelled, measure, rash, constitution.

- Waiver, convey, orchestrate, abundance, duke.

- Restrict, paint, manoeuvre, doggerel, outpouring.

- Strict, type, reunite, display, graft.

- Scales, disgruntled, hallowed, mastery, titan.

- Air, elimination, disarray, linen, acai.

- Wood, deluge, prop, vindicate, acetate.

- Earth, deluxe, jarred, syndicate, accessory.

NOTES

MUSICAL INTERLUDE
PART SIX

- Shut Up And Dance – Walk The Moon.
- Last Train To Clarksville – The Monkees.
- Smoke On The Water – Deep Purple.
- A Sky Full Of Stars – Coldplay.
- Video Killed The Radio Star – The Buggles.
- Johnny B Goode – Chuck Berry.
- Laugh Now, Cry Later – Drake.

- Ever Fallen In Love (With Someone You Shouldn't Have)? – The Buzzcocks.

- Catch A Falling Star – Perry Como.

- Delete Forever – Grimes.

- Do I Love You? – The Ronettes.

- Goodbye Stranger – Supertramp.

- Cartoon Heroes – Aqua.

- The Colours Of My Life – Micheal Crawford.

- Sweet Talking Guy – The Chiffons.

- Don't Call Me Baby – Madison Avenue.

- Iron Out The Rough Spots – Paul Young.
- Son Of A Preacher Man – Dusty Springfield.
- This Years Love – David Gray.
- More Than A Feeling – Boston.
- Virtual Insanity – Jamiroquai.
- I Will Survive – Gloria Gaynor.
- The Deadwood Stage – Doris Day.
- Good Riddance (Time Of Your Life) – Green Day.
- Forever Young – Alphaville.

- Johnny Angel –
  Shelley Fabares.
- Torn – Natalie Imbruglia.
- Hang on Sloopy –
  The McCoys.
- Down Under – Men At Work.
- Car Wash – Rose Royce.
- All Rise – Blue.
- Soul Man – Sam And Dave.
- Baker Street –
  Gerry Rafferty.

COMMONLY CONFUSED WORDS
PART SIX

Write something for each set of words using them all correctly

Moral and morale

Moral relates to principles of right and wrong in human behaviour.

Morale refers to enthusiasm and loyalty of a person or group towards a task.

Eminent and imminent

Eminent means successful, well-known, and respected.

Imminent means happening very soon.

Bridal and bridle

Bridal refers to things connected with a bride or wedding.

Bridle fits on a horse's head so it can be guided or can mean to react in an angry way.

STRENGTHEN YOUR WORDS
PART SIX

Write a sentence using the first word, then replace that word with the second one.

INSTEAD OF	TRY
Safe	Harmless
Fake	Fabricate
Cry	Weep
Happy	Cheerful
Shy	Bashful
Tired	Weary
Dirty	Filthy
Clean	Spotless

Shout	Roar
Hurt	Injured
Colour	Hue

THIS MIGHT HELP
PART SIX

- Imagine you have magic powers. What would they be and how would you use them?

- Think of a TV show, film or book and rewrite the ending.

- Make up new words to a tune you know well.

- Take a character and write a new story about them.

- Imagine a story you know well as a different genre.

- Use your non dominant hand to do something.

- Create titles for books by another author.

- Write about your day as if you were a different person.
- If you had the power to grant wishes whose wishes would you grant and what do you think they would be?
- Observe the sky every day for a week and see if you can predict the weather.
- Ask someone what they remember about a place they have visited or an event they have witnessed.
- Find prompts on social media.
- Use this book.

FRIENDS' PROMPTS
PART SIX

"I can't trust the accuracy of my memories anymore, but I remember my reaction to the painting very clearly. I couldn't forget it if I tried, because I thought it was the most exquisitely beautiful thing I had ever seen. Now I can't bear to look at it."

Journeys: The Archers of Saint Sebastian – Jeanne Roland

"The morbid painted figure staring past me, eyes glazed with pain, is more than a gruesome reminder. It's an accusation, a riddle I can't solve."

Journeys: The Archers of Saint Sebastian – Jeanne Roland

"Rats can be awfully hard to catch," Remy's saying slowly, a little frown on his face.

"They're such clever creatures, aren't they Marek? Only eventually, they outsmart themselves."

I look up, to find disconcertingly that Remy's looking right at me. I can only imagine what I must look like.

"Yes, they outsmart themselves," he repeats slowly. "They make a mistake. And when they do, then you catch them."

Squires: The Archers of Saint Sebastian II – Jeanne Roland

"He knows exactly what I'm asking, the lousy, magnificent bastard. He's just going to make me say it."

Squires: The Archers of Saint Sebastian II – Jeanne Roland

“He’s damned observant, for a dead man.”

Squires: The Archers of Saint Sebastian II – Jeanne Roland

“In my experience, nothing good ever happens in gazebos.”

Masters: The Archers of Saint Sebastian III – Jeanne Roland

“… if I’m to succeed this year, I’ve got to learn a lesson from my enemies. This year, I’ll be the boy who knows how to bide his time.”

Masters: The Archers of Saint Sebastian III – Jeanne Roland

“Vengeance isn’t my style, but I guess I’m going to have to get used to it.”

Guards: The Archers of Saint Sebastian IV – Jeanne Roland

"It's not just that vengeance isn't my style. As it turns out, I'm not very good at it."

Guards: The Archers of Saint Sebastian IV – Jeanne Roland

"Six will die. One will get vengeance."

Six Must Die: A Seven Against Thebes retelling, WIP – Jeanne Roland

"I lived my life in the Technicolor of youth ... "

Just Take Five – A Contemporary Poetry Collection – Karen Honnor

"Frost dusted fragility strung across the gate, delicate, deliberate, a wonder."

Just Take Five – A Contemporary Poetry Collection – Karen Honnor

"Sadness pervaded as her gaze fell onto her thin hands and she moved her fingers slowly up and down, mirroring a silent melody line that they used to play somewhere before. Somewhere where the spotlight shone and glasses clinked in camaraderie."

Unravelling - A Tale of Strength, Love and Dementia – Karen Honnor

"Though the sisters made the best of such tasks, they much preferred the work that took them outside. The early morning forage for mushrooms when the dew clung to the blades of grass and an ethereal mist hung over the fields and they could pretend that they were the only ones left on the planet. Even Lillian could be still and silent for a while when they stood listening to the birdsong and watching the dawn lighting the touch paper of another day."

Unravelling - A Tale of Strength, Love and Dementia –
Karen Honnor

"I'm a car with no throttle as it takes the bend,
An email deleted when I should have pressed send,
Like a song with no rhythm or tune to hear,
A woman alone at the end of a pier ... "

Diary of a Dizzy Peri - Poems and thoughts on midlife, menopause and mental health. –
Karen Honnor

"I had a dream the other night of Polaroids and petals,
Both were strewn across clean sheets, beautifully fragile."

Polaroids and Petals – Karen Honnor

"Now Billy counts his buttons,
Though he only has a few,
He lines them up across his bed,
Does not have much else to do.

No-one comes to visit now,
Which he doesn't understand,
So Billy counts his buttons
And holds them in his hand."

Click and Connect – A Collection of Hope – Karen Honnor

"The lesson I suppose, is to make the most of your time: sing, dance, laugh, walk up a hill together and take photos to share - not of stuff, Instagram meals and landscapes, but of people who matter, all of them and get some of them printed off too. For on a rainy weekend in the future, your children, or grandchildren, will love rummaging through a box of old photos and sharing in little nostalgic glimpses of people, places and times that were otherwise forgotten."

Have you heard the ocean soundtrack play its symphony of hues whilst woven threads of glowing pink entice the sun to slowly sink and scatter twilight wishes to the moon?

Finding My Way - 2nd Edition. – Karen Honnor

Now you've read my book
don't forget to review
Amazon, Goodreads,
Bookbub too!
Thank you very much
I'm counting on you!

Lily x

ACKNOWLEDGEMENTS

Thank you for reading this book. I hope you were inspired to be creative.

Thank you to my guest contributors –

Alethea Lyons, Alexandra Peel, Cheryl Burman, Eve Koguce, Heather Lynn, J. M. Langan, Jeanne Roland, Jessica Ungeheuer, J. C. Paulson, K. L. Small, K. T. McGivens, Karen Honnor, Ken Paulson, P. S. C. Willis, Rue Sparks, R. E. Loten, Tanya Packer, Tessa Barrie and Vastine Bondurant.

This book has been a long time coming. I am grateful to those who have read, advised and cheered me on throughout that time.

Thanks so much to Jo, Cin, Mel and Thea.

Thanks to Christine who has put up with me forever.

My thanks, as always, to Butterfly who has flown with me every day since before my first book was published.

My thanks to all who follow and support me in any way, be that online or off.

I am grateful for all of you.

BY THE AUTHOR

Poetry Books

My Fathers Daughter
A Taste of What's to Come
Rainbow's Red Book of Poetry
Rainbow's Orange Book of Poetry
Rainbow's Yellow Book of Poetry

Short Stories

Sandcastles

Kids' Books

Santa's Early Christmas
The Palm Tree Swingers
Island Band
If I Were Invisible…
Christmas Capers

Lily's Amazon

SANDCASTLES
short stories
LILY LAWSON

MY FATHER'S
DAUGHTER
LILY LAWSON

A TASTE
OF WHAT'S
TO COME
LILY LAWSON

RAINBOW'S
RED
BOOK
OF
POETRY
lily lawson

RAINBOW'S
ORANGE
BOOK
OF
POETRY
lily lawson

RAINBOW'S
YELLOW
BOOK
OF
POETRY
lily lawson

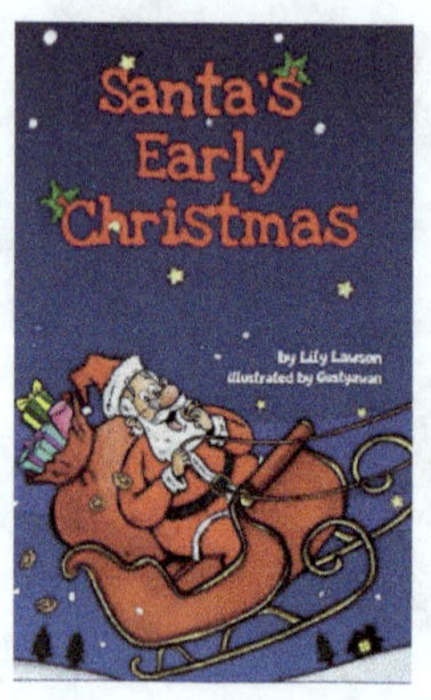
Santa's Early Christmas
by Lily Lawson
illustrated by Gustyawan

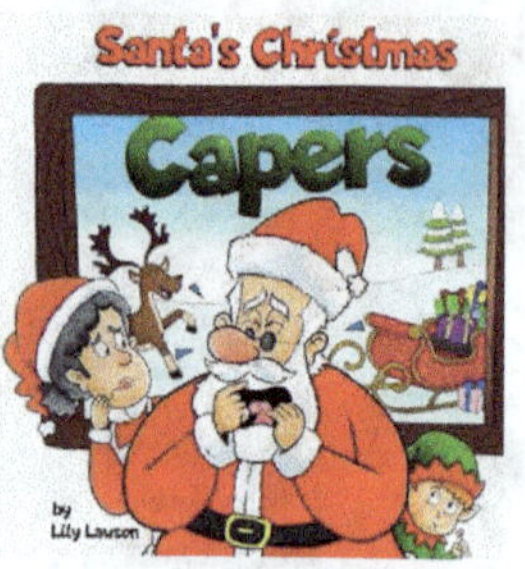
Santa's Christmas
Capers
by
Lily Lawson

IF I WERE
INVISIBLE
By Lily Lawson
Illustrated by Gustyawan

THE PALM TREE
SWINGERS ISLAND BAND
By Lily Lawson
Illustrated by Gustyawan

ABOUT THE AUTHOR

Lily Lawson is a poet
and writer living in the UK.
She has poetry, short stories,
and creative non-fiction
published in anthologies
and online in addition to her books

You can find out more about Lily
and read more of her work
on her blog.

You can follow her on Amazon
where you will find her books.

FRIENDS' BIOS

Alethea Lyons

Alethea (ze/she) is the author of the supernatural dark fantasy *Seer of York series,* published by Brigids Gate Press. She has also written the folkloric cyberfae novel *Legend of the Bard*.

Her short stories can be found in a variety of publications.

Alethea lives in Manchester, UK with zir husband, little Sprite, a cacophony of stringed instruments, and more tea than ze can drink in a lifetime.

https://linktr.ee/alethearlyons (Books/Social Media)

Greater Manchester Events Organiser for the British Fantasy Society

https://alethealyons.com/

Author of the Seer of York series (Brigids Gate Press)

Alexandra Peel

Alexandra Peel was born in the North West of England, where she now works in education; she has a background in Fine Art and is a Learning Support Practitioner. She lives with her husband of thirty-five years.

Her stories have been featured in a variety of anthologies. She is a self-published author of the science-fiction fantasy novel, *Haft*, the Steampunk duology, *Beneath the Skin*, and more.

She has also written two contemporary novellas under the name E. V. Faulkner.

Alexandra loves foreign films, gardening, foamy bananas and gin. She has an abhorrence of pulses.

https://us.amazon.com/Books-Alexandra-Peel/s?rh=n%3A283155%2Cp_27%3AAlexandra%2BPeel

https://www.sticksandstonesbooks.com/

https://linktr.ee/alexandra.peel

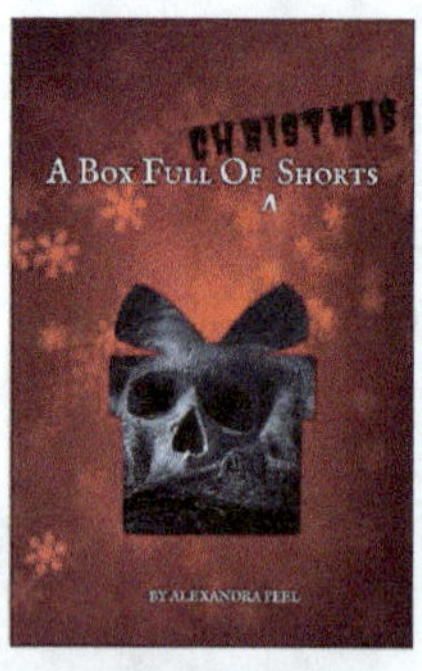

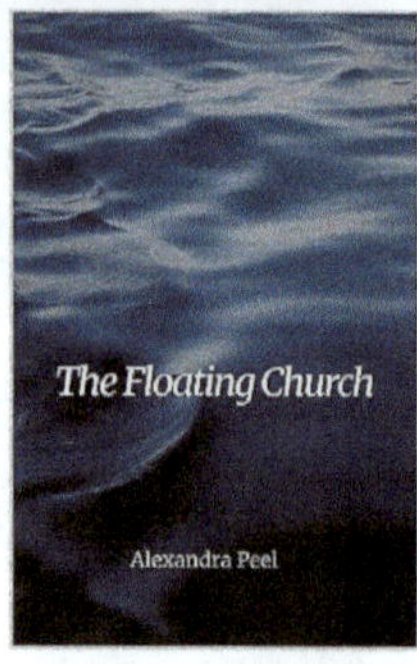

Cheryl Burman

Cheryl Burman lives in the Forest of Dean, UK, with her husband where she is continually inspired by the trees.

She is a multi-genre author of middle grade fantasy, women's fiction and historical fantasy.

Her flash fiction, short stories, and whole or parts of her novels have won awards, and several appear in various anthologies.

https://cherylburman.com/

https://www.facebook.com/Cheryl BurmanAuthor

http://mybook.to/RiverWitch

https://mybook.to/WinteroftheWhiteHorde

Eve Koguce

Eve had spent fifteen years, trying to fit into the office work pattern.

Despite feeling miserable and out of place every day of that climbing-the-ladder process, she managed to build a relatively successful career after an ambitious shift from the private to the public sector.

She worked with internationally funded projects and met people from all over the world every day. But it failed to ignite a spark in her heart.

After her son was born, she had a unique chance to stop and rethink not only what she'd achieved so far, but what she really wanted from life.

She made a decision to leave her old life behind, and she has never regretted it.

Eve lives in the seaside town Jurmala in Latvia, Northern Europe, with her husband, her son, and their two ginger cats.

https://evekoguce.com/

https://www.instagram.com/eve_koguce_books/

mybook.to/xYy9viy (Tangle of Choices)

Heather Lynn

Heather Lynn, born in Toronto, Ontario, lives with her family just north of the city.

Her education in biology and health sciences has supported an ongoing interest in physiology and the potential of herbal healing.

In addition, she has been intrigued by the possibility and impossibility of time travel since childhood.

When she's not writing, Heather enjoys family time, working in her garden, and learning more about the 'power' of stones.

https://www.HeatherLynnBooks.com

https://linktr.ee/HeatherLynn_author

http://mybook.to/SkyWatcher

J. M. Langan

J. M. Langan is a Shropshire lass and adopted Brummie bab. She is fuelled by coffee, cats and a husband who mutters, 'Be productive,' before she disappears into her loft bedroom to imagine worlds and then write them down.

On social media, she is known as MuddyNoSugar, which is how she takes her coffee, and a nickname which emerged during a game of Texas hold 'em back in the olden times before kids. There's probably a story in there somewhere…

https://muddynosugar.wordpress.com/

https://www.castlepriorypress.com/

https://mybook.to/AboutCharlie

https://mybook.to/SolsticeBaby

Jeanne Roland

Roland hails from California, where she spent most of her youth lounging at the pool, soaking up the sun, and daydreaming. She had a key ring that read 'I'm running away to join the circus,' and her favourite moment of the day was when the local movie theatre went dark, and the slogan 'escape to the movies' appeared on the screen.

As an adult, her passions include all things melodramatic and beautiful – everything from classic movies, poetry: ancient tragedy and epic, to Italian opera.

She now lives in small midwestern town with her Greek husband, her fraternal twins, and a Bernese mountain dog named Franco Corelli.

https://jeanneroland.com/

https://mybook.to/MyArchersSeries

https://www.facebook.com/jeannerolandwrites

Jessica Ungeheuer

Jessica Ungeheuer (she/her) is a writer and artist. While earning her visual arts and digital media degree she studied creative writing and screenwriting.

Her favourite genres to read and write are dystopian sci fi and horror.

She lives in sunny Bradenton Florida with her husband, son, and two mischievous cats.

You can find her artwork and other stories on her socials through her linktr.ee/JessicaUWriting, or on Twitter/X and Instagram https://www.instagram.com/phoenixfire110/

https://books2read.com/u/mV1V1J

Joanne (J. C.) Paulson

Joanne (J.C.) Paulson, a long-time Canadian journalist, has been published in newspapers and magazines for longer than she would care to admit.

About nine years ago, her unquiet brain demanded change, and she shifted (partly) from fact to fiction.

She is the author of a mystery series including the novels *Adam's Witness, Broken Through, Fire Lake, Griffin's Cure,* and *Two Hundred Bones*, a novella. *The Maddox Verdict*, the sixth and final book in the main arc of the series, is coming in Spring 2026.

She has also written a historical fiction/western novel entitled *Blood and Dust*, published by Black Rose Writing, and a wee children's book, *Magic Mack and The Mischief-Makers*.

https://substack.com/@joannepaulson (Frantic Scribe)

https://www.facebook.com/jcpaulsonauthor

https://www.jcpaulsonwriter.com/books

https://amzn.to/2V6a6mM (Amazon Author Page)

K. L. Small

K. L. Small writes timeless stories of wonder. She lives in Florida on a ranch called Carousel Acres, with her husband, two horses, four cats, and assorted wildlife.

Her website is https://kathleenlsmall.com, where readers can subscribe to her monthly newsletter.

https://www.facebook.com/KLSFantasy/

https://a.co/d/7i4BWOk (Letters from Shadow Oaks)

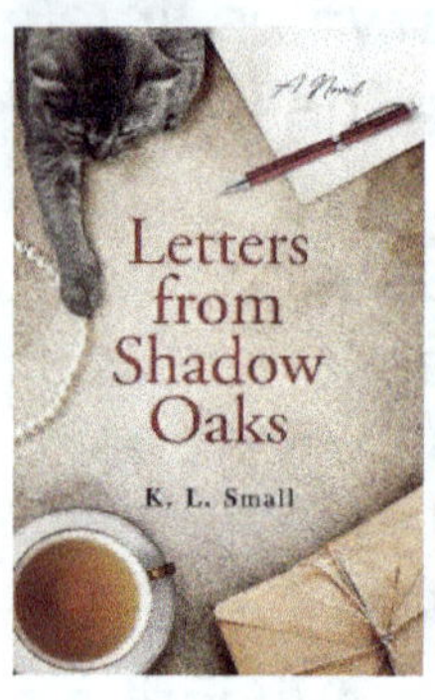

K. T. McGivens

K. T. McGivens is an award-winning American poet and cozy mystery author of *The Katie Porter Mystery Series.*

She started her working life as a public school teacher and also taught on the college level before transferring to a career in healthcare where she specialized in dementia care for senior citizens.

She has a Bachelor's Degree in Education and a Master's Degree in Healthcare Administration. She lives in Florida and has two grown children.

The Secret at Sunset Hill (https://mybook.to/XhW0)

The Passing of Preston Peabody (https://mybook.to/Y45gMSk)

The Incident on Ivory Island (https://mybook.to/1sJ6wDF)

The Ransom for Ruth Reed (https://mybook.to/0qM0waA)

The Traveler on the Train (https://mybook.to/hnWzfy)

https://www.katieportermysteryseries.com/

https://www.facebook.com/Katieportermysteries

K.T. MCGIVENS
THE SECRET AT
SUNSET HILL
A KATIE PORTER MYSTERY -1-

K. T. MCGIVENS
THE
PASSING
OF
PRESTON
PEABODY
A Katie Porter Mystery
Book 7

K. T. MCGIVENS
THE
INCIDENT
ON
IVORY
ISLAND
A Katie Porter Mystery
Book 10

K. T. MCGIVENS
THE
RANSOM
FOR
RUTH REED
A Katie Porter Mystery
Book 15

K.T. MCGIVENS
THE
TRAVELER
ON THE
TRAIN
A KATIE PORTER MYSTERY
BOOK 20

Karen Honnor

Karen Honnor has been playing with words for a long time now. Mostly focused on her poetry and script writing in the past, she long harboured a desire to create something more significant.

Motherhood and a busy teaching career left little time for that, but then circumstances would see her leaving the classroom in 2018 and giving herself the space to see where her pen could lead her.

Now, Karen devotes her time to writing and to her family, baking, gardening and regular dog walks where being close to nature helps to bring an inner calm.

Her writing journey continues with seven books now published – a memoir, historical fiction novella and five poetry works. After all, she is a poet at heart.

Her blog and writing updates can be found on her
website: www.karenhonnor.com

https://linktr.ee/karenhonnor

https://mybook.to/G6Vy
Click and Connect

https://mybook.to/a9O7L
Diary of a Dizzy Peri

https://mybook.to/4SdzB
Finding My Way

https://mybook.to/5Npwoin
Just Take Five

https://mybook.to/axSp Polaroids and Petals

https://mybook.to/Fr23R9L
Unravelling

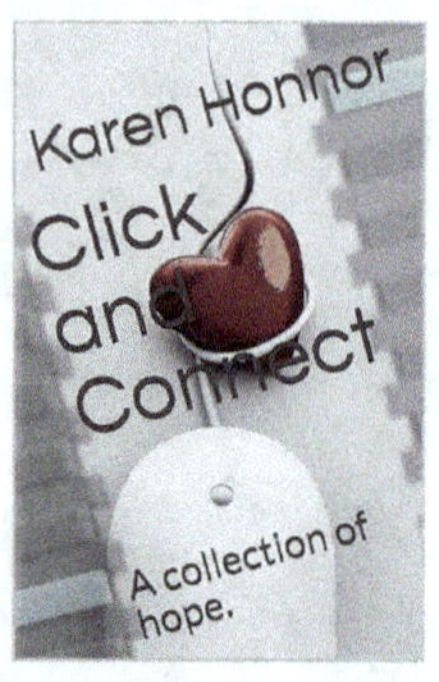
Karen Honnor
Click and Connect
A collection of hope.

DIARY OF A DIZZY PERI
KAREN HONNOR

KAREN HONNOR
2nd Edition
FINDING MY WAY

A CONTEMPORARY POETRY COLLECTION
JUST TAKE FIVE
KAREN HONNOR

POLAROIDS AND PETALS
KAREN HONNOR

A Tale of Strength, Love and Dementia
UNRAVELLING
KAREN HONNOR

Ken Paulson

Ken Paulson is a goldsmith and business owner in Saskatoon, Canada, aka the Paris of the Prairies. His profession largely defines him, so that's what he primarily writes about.

He is the author of The Goldsmith Book and Frogs and Alarm Clocks, a memoir.

Ken is married to journalist and author J. C. Paulson, whom he partly credits for publishing his own work.

An eclectic soul, he likes to take pictures, but is not a photographer. He likes playing guitar and harmonica, but is not a musician. And he likes to write, but is not an author. Oh, wait. Apparently, he is.

https://www.amazon.ca/stores/Ken-Paulson/author/B071X9GZD3

https://www.amazon.com/Frogs-Alarm-Clocks-Darkish-Memoir-ebook/dp/B0DK5XCWCB

https://mybook.to/Aevy

https://mybook.to/FrogsAndAlarmClocks

P. S. C. Willis

P.S.C. Willis is a queer British author living abroad, where they are an active member of the local writing scene and the LGBTQIA+ community.

They have previously been published in DreamForge Magazine and multiple short story anthologies.

Their debut novel *Crying Out for Magic* was published by Space Wizard Press and is available wherever you buy books.

They like to create stories that allow others to believe in good people, in magic, or both.

Find out more about them at pscwillis.com

https://pscwillis.substack.com/

https://www.instagram.com/pscwillis/

https://www.spacewizardsciencefantasy.com/book/crying-out-for-magic

Rue Sparks

Rue Sparks is a composite of neurosis and nonsense held together by duct tape and sheer stubbornness.

A widow, disabled, and queer, they traverse the equally harsh and cathartic landscape where trauma and healing align to create stories that burrow into the hearts and minds of their readers.

They live in a rural Michigan town surrounded by forest on all sides so that they can opt out of humanity at will.

https://www.ruesparks.com/

http://www.patreon.com/archetypeproject

https://books2read.com/thefableofwren

Ruth (R. E.) Loten/Henrietta Edwards

Ruth's first writing memory is for her writer's badge in Brownies but her MA in Creative Writing probably trumps that.

Ruth is the co-founder and director of the publishing company Castle Priory Press and was Writer In Residence at Brightlingsea Lido from 2021-2024.

In January 2025, she moved to become Writer In Residence at the Thames Estuary Lobster Hatchery.

Ruth publishes adult books under her own name including a short fiction collection, *Words Will Travel.*

Her children's books including *The Courts series* are published under the pen name Henrietta Edwards. She has also been published in various anthologies, helping to edit many of them as well.

The Rise of the Winter Queen, the next book in The Courts series is coming soon.

https://www.reloten.com/

https://www.castlepriorypress.com/

https://www.amazon.co.uk/dp/B09YVFWTZQ

(The Reign of the Winter King)
https://mybook.to/LotenUnforgettable

The Reign of the Winter King
The Courts Book 1
Henrietta Edwards

Unforgettable
R.E. Loten

Tanya Packer

One Thanksgiving, Tanya was blessed with the birth of her handsome son, and she started telling him stories.

As she whispered stories to him and they played with his Lego figures, the desire to write was rekindled. Eventually, she began writing stories for him.

Discussions with her family led to yet more writing adventures.

Tanya is an active member of the Society of Children's Book Writers and Illustrators and active with the online writing community.

She has a Master of Divinity where she specialized in educational ministries.

The inspiration for her books comes from working with families and young people for over fifteen years and from her love of classical works *like Narnia, Lord of the Rings, Mary Poppins, Neverending Story, Bridge to Terabithia, The Magic School Bus,* and *Labyrinth.*

https://tanyapacker.com/about/

https://www.facebook.com/TanyaPackersbooks

http://author.to/TanyaPackerbooks

Tessa Barrie

Tessa Barrie is the alter ego of Sally Edmondson.

Born in Yorkshire, with Greek blood running through her veins, she lives in Jersey, Channel Islands, UK, where she plans to grow old disgracefully.

Having started writing novels in later life means there is no time to sit around procrastinating –- she needs to get on with it. So she can generally be found writing unless overwhelmed by a sudden guilt-induced flurry of housework, either at home in Jersey or at her happy place in Portugal.

http://www.tessabarrie.com/

https://www.facebook.com/TessaBarrieAuthor

https://www.amazon.co.uk/Tessa-Barrie/e/B096RQ62YG

Vastine Bondurant

Author. Half of the Vastine and Marty Podcast Team. Blogger. Reader. Lover of Music: Classical, Big Band, Swing, Jazz, Rock and Roll. Texas Girl. Dreamer and Lover of all things historical.

She loves to read and write stories of romance, the sizzling chemistry that draws people together. The passion. In other words…a lover of ROMANCE! She can't get enough of the stuff!

https://vastinebondurant.blogspot.com/

https://www.facebook.com/profile.php?id=61551569531224

https://t.co/rj3vZTXrru (Joseph's Coat)

www.ingramcontent.com/pod-product-compliance
Lightning Source LLC
LaVergne TN
LVHW020053110826
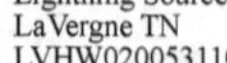
845155LV00022B/79

9781916278097